COLLINS

PICTURE ATLAS

Written by
Marit Claridge

Illustrated by
Stephen Holmes

NOTE TO PARENTS AND TEACHERS

This book provides a fascinating introduction to maps and atlases.
The emphasis is on giving an overall idea of what each country is like
physically, what its buildings look like, what animals live there, and
what its people do, rather than on exact maps which show precise
positions of towns and borders.

In a rapidly changing world national borders often change between
reprints: this atlas is up-to-date at the time of going to press, but
readers should be aware of recent changes.

CONTENTS

42

14

20

12

16

22

18

30

38

36

26

24

28

32

34

44

43

40

Introduction

This is a book of maps of the countries of the world. On pages 6-11 there are three different maps showing the whole world. The first shows where the rivers, mountains, oceans, plains and plateaus are, the second shows what kinds of plants and animals there are around the world and the third shows the positions of all the countries in the world.

Following the world maps, there are more detailed maps of different parts of the world. You can find out which page each map is on by looking at the contents list on page 2 – the map at the bottom of the list also gives the page numbers. At the end of the book there is an index. This index is a list of the names of countries and main towns in alphabetical order. Next to each name there is a page number or numbers which is where the places can be found in the book.

On this and the next two pages, you can find out more about maps and how to use the maps in this book.

About our world

Our world is the planet earth. It is one of 9 planets which circle around the sun. The earth is shaped like a ball, which is slightly flattened at the top and bottom. Most of the earth, about 70%, is covered by sea and the rest is land. The land on earth is in seven main patches, which are called continents.
Imagine holding a small model of the earth in your hands. If you turned it round you would be able to see the continents, as in the pictures below.

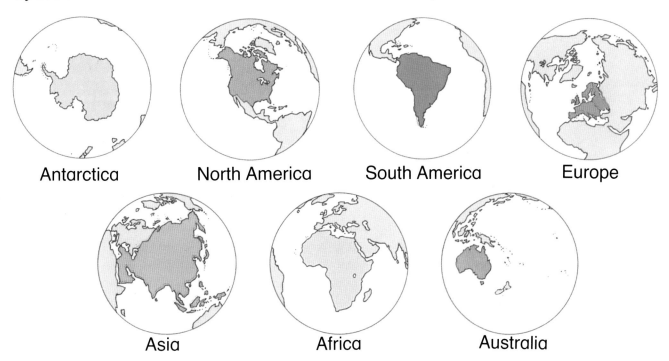

Antarctica   North America   South America   Europe

Asia   Africa   Australia

Countries of the world

The world has been divided up into countries by people. A country is a land which has its own people, money and laws. It usually has its own flag as well – the flags for most countries are shown on the maps on pages 12-45. The boundaries between different countries are shown by pink lines on the maps.

Making maps of the world

As the earth is ball-shaped, the best kind of world map to show the correct shape of the continents is a ball-shaped one too. Maps shaped like balls are called globes. With a globe you can only see part of the world at one time. Map makers have also made flat maps of the world so that we can see it all at the same time in a book like this one you are reading, called an atlas.

Countries which are islands are bordered by the sea. If you tavel from one country to another you will usually need a passport. Most of the world's continents are divided into many countries but Australia is just one large country, and Antarctica is a little different because nobody lives there except for scientists.

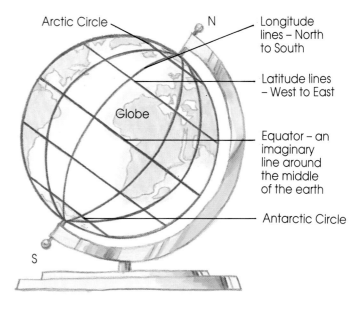

Arctic Circle

N

Longitude lines – North to South

Latitude lines – West to East

Globe

Equator – an imaginary line around the middle of the earth

Antarctic Circle

S

Peeling an orange

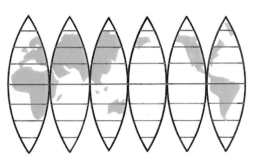

Peeling the world

When you try to draw a flat map of our ball-shaped world, some parts get stretched out of shape while other parts get squashed up. Imagine the earth is an orange. If you peel off the skin and try to lie it flat, you can see the difficulty that map makers have. Map makers have to

change the shapes of countries slightly to make the maps flat so they can be printed on a page. The different ways of making maps flat are called projections and they can vary a lot. Map makers use imaginary lines on the earth to help them position places accurately within each projection.

The maps in this book

Most of the maps cover two pages, for example Japan is on pages 36 and 37 and Africa is on pages 28 and 29. Africa is much bigger than Japan even though they take up the same space in the book. If you want to know how big one country is in comparison to another, look at the world map on pages 10 and 11.

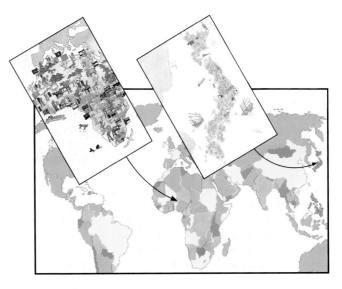

Things to look out for

The maps in this book have small pictures on them which show the kind of countryside and where different things, such as coffee, grow around the world. Each map is very small compared to the size of the real world, so these pictures are signs to give you the general idea rather than showing exactly where everything is. Some of the signs appear on several of the maps. It will be obvious to you what most of them mean but some are not so obvious and they are in the list opposite.

National flags have been placed near most of the capital cities. Names of the countries and capital cities are both in capital letters.

Some of the flags are shown flying backwards, with the pole on the right. If you copy these flags, remember to draw them the other way round.

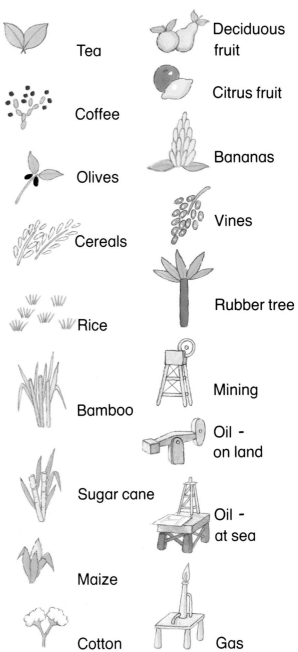

Tea

Coffee

Olives

Cereals

Rice

Bamboo

Sugar cane

Maize

Cotton

Deciduous fruit

Citrus fruit

Bananas

Vines

Rubber tree

Mining

Oil - on land

Oil - at sea

Gas

Physical World Map

This map of the world shows where the world's main mountains, plateaus, plains, oceans, rivers and lakes are. You can see from this map that there are mountain ranges in the sea as well as on the land. The deepest parts of the sea are long, narrow trenches.

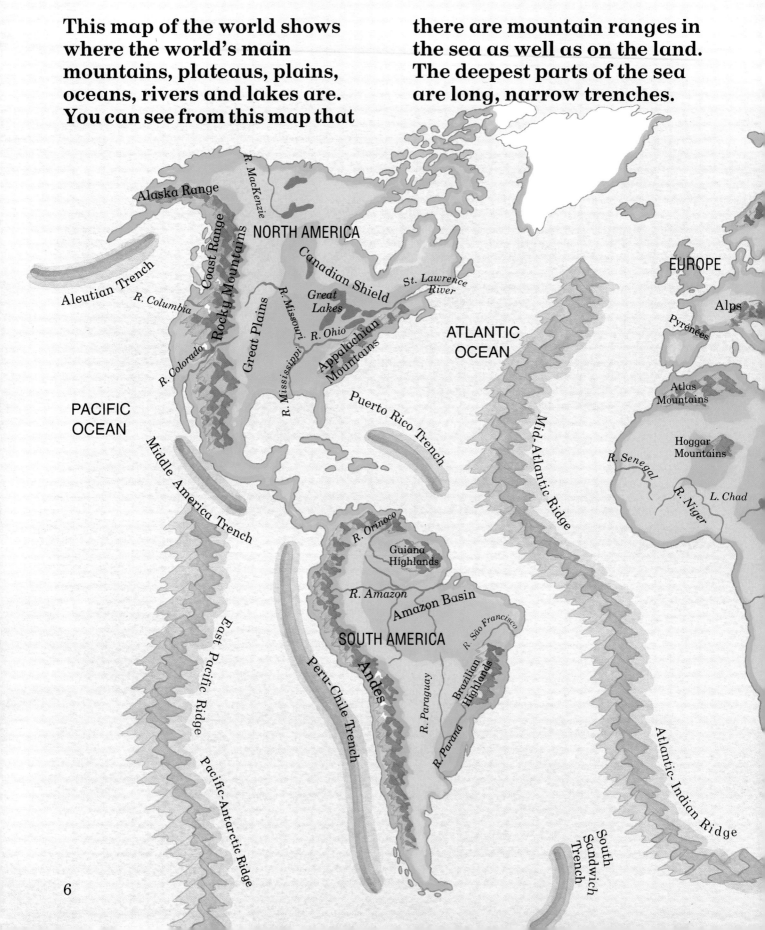

Alaska Range

R. MacKenzie

Aleutian Trench

Coast Range

R. Columbia

Rocky Mountains

NORTH AMERICA

Canadian Shield

Great Lakes

Great Plains

R. Missouri

R. Ohio

R. Colorado

R. Mississippi

Appalachian Mountains

St. Lawrence River

PACIFIC OCEAN

ATLANTIC OCEAN

Puerto Rico Trench

Middle America Trench

EUROPE

Alps

Pyrenees

Atlas Mountains

Hoggar Mountains

R. Senegal

R. Niger

L. Chad

Mid-Atlantic Ridge

East Pacific Ridge

Pacific-Antarctic Ridge

R. Orinoco

Guiana Highlands

R. Amazon

Amazon Basin

SOUTH AMERICA

Andes

Peru-Chile Trench

R. Paraguay

R. Paraná

R. São Francisco

Brazilian Highlands

Atlantic-Indian Ridge

South Sandwich Trench

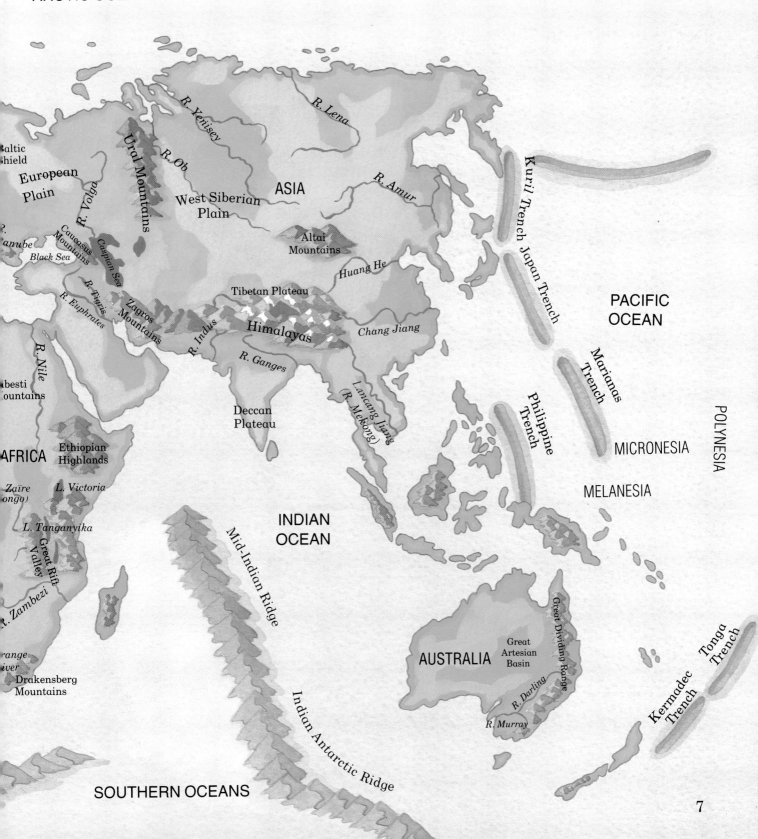

ARCTIC OCEAN

Baltic
Shield

European
Plain

Ural Mountains

R. Yenisey

R. Ob

R. Lena

R. Amur

ASIA

West Siberian
Plain

R. Volga

Caucasus
Mountains

Black Sea

Caspian Sea

Altai
Mountains

Huang He

R. Danube

R. Tigris

R. Euphrates

Zagros
Mountains

Tibetan Plateau

Himalayas

Chang Jiang

R. Indus

R. Ganges

R. Nile

Tibesti
Mountains

Deccan
Plateau

Lancang Jiang
(R. Mekong)

AFRICA

Ethiopian
Highlands

Zaire
(Congo)

L. Victoria

L. Tanganyika

Great Rift Valley

R. Zambezi

INDIAN
OCEAN

Mid-Indian Ridge

Orange
River

Drakensberg
Mountains

Indian Antarctic Ridge

AUSTRALIA

Great
Artesian
Basin

Great Dividing Range

R. Darling

R. Murray

Kuril Trench

Japan Trench

PACIFIC
OCEAN

Marianas
Trench

Philippine
Trench

MICRONESIA

MELANESIA

POLYNESIA

Kermadec
Trench

Tonga
Trench

SOUTHERN OCEANS

World Environments

The kind of plants and animals around the world depend on what sort of climate the area has – how hot, cold, wet or dry it is. They are also affected by the kind of soil, whether the land is flat or hilly and by farming and towns. Together these things make up areas called environments, where particular kinds of plants and animals live.

This map gives a general idea of where the eight main environments in the world are. In some of these environments the wild plants and animals no longer exist because people have farmed the land and built huge cities.

Each environment is shown by a different colour. Match the colours on the map to the boxes around the edge to find out more about them.

DESERT
In these areas there is little or no rain. Most deserts are very hot in the day and cold at night. The only plants are scrubby bushes or cactuses. The desert is the home of lizards and snakes and small mammals such as gerbils which burrow under the ground.

MEDITERRANEAN WOODLAND
These areas have hot, dry summers and warm, wet winters. They contain evergreen trees and shrubs, such as stone-pine, olive trees and lavender. Lizards live here and sometimes wild pigs are found in the scrubland.

TUNDRA

Tundra is found in arctic areas. The soil below the surface is frozen all the time. Mosses and lichens are the main plants with mammals and birds such as lemmings, ptarmigan, reindeer and Arctic foxes.

GRASSLAND

In these areas there are hot summers and cold winters. The grasslands are grazed by wild animals such as bison, antelopes, wild horses, and, in Australia, kangaroos.

SAVANNA

These are grasslands found in hot areas with mainly summer rainfall. There are some trees, such as the acacia tree. The grasslands are the home of many animals such as giraffes, zebras, rhinoceroses, lions, cheetahs, and leopards.

CONIFEROUS FOREST

These are forests in cold areas. They contain trees such as pine, fir, spruce and larch. Many wild animals live in the forests, such as bears, foxes, wolves and elks (a large deer).

WOODLAND

These are areas of mild climate. The woodlands are made up of trees such as oak, beech, ash and, in Australia, gum trees. Deer, badgers and pheasants are some of the creatures that live in most of the woodlands.

TROPICAL RAINFORESTS

Tropical rainforest is found around the equator where it is hot and wet all year round. There are many different kinds of trees and flowers and creatures such as monkeys and parrots. Above the trees, butterflies and birds live in the sunlight.

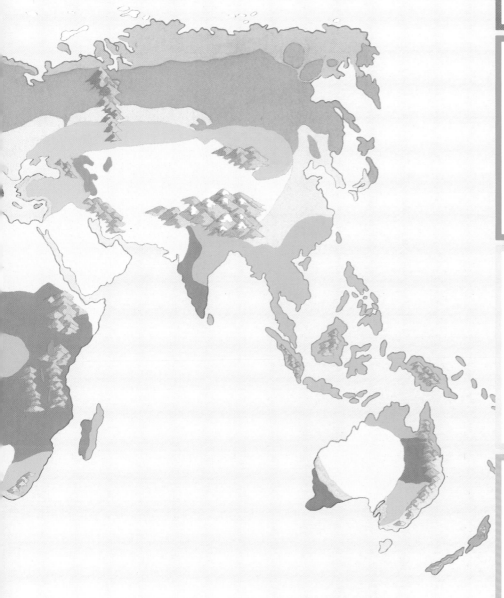

Countries of the World

This map shows the positions of the countries of the world. Some of the countries are so small that the names do not fit. These countries are numbered. You can look up the numbers, to see which countries they are, in the lists around the page.

1 BELIZE
2 GUATEMALA
3 HONDURAS
4 EL SALVADOR
5 NICARAGUA
6 COSTA RICA
7 PANAMA
8 JAMAICA
9 HAITI
10 DOMINICAN REPUBLIC
11 CUBA
12 ANTIGUA & BARBUDA
13 BARBADOS
14 DOMINICA
15 GRENADA
16 ST KITTS-NEVIS
17 ST LUCIA
18 ST VINCENT & THE GRENADINES
19 TRINIDAD AND TOBAGO
20 GUYANA
21 SURINAM
22 FRENCH GUIANA
23 DENMARK
24 THE NETHERLANDS
25 BELGIUM
26 LUXEMBOURG
27 GERMANY
28 LIECHTENSTEIN
29 SWITZERLAND
30 ANDORRA
31 MONACO
32 VATICAN CITY

33 MALTA
34 SAN MARINO
35 AUSTRIA
36 CZECH REPUBLIC
37 SLOVAKIA
38 HUNGARY
39 SLOVENIA
40 CROATIA
41 BOSNIA-HERZEGOVINA
42 YUGOSLAVIA
43 ALBANIA
44 BULGARIA
45 ROMANIA
46 MOLDOVA
47 POLAND
48 LITHUANIA
49 LATVIA
50 ESTONIA

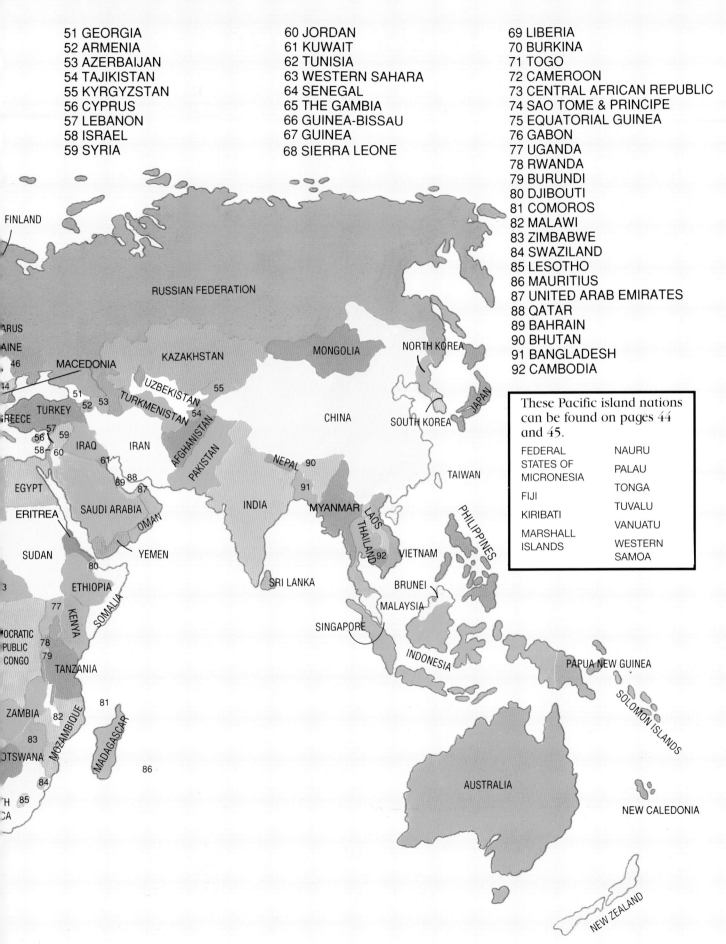

51 GEORGIA
52 ARMENIA
53 AZERBAIJAN
54 TAJIKISTAN
55 KYRGYZSTAN
56 CYPRUS
57 LEBANON
58 ISRAEL
59 SYRIA

60 JORDAN
61 KUWAIT
62 TUNISIA
63 WESTERN SAHARA
64 SENEGAL
65 THE GAMBIA
66 GUINEA-BISSAU
67 GUINEA
68 SIERRA LEONE

69 LIBERIA
70 BURKINA
71 TOGO
72 CAMEROON
73 CENTRAL AFRICAN REPUBLIC
74 SAO TOME & PRINCIPE
75 EQUATORIAL GUINEA
76 GABON
77 UGANDA
78 RWANDA
79 BURUNDI
80 DJIBOUTI
81 COMOROS
82 MALAWI
83 ZIMBABWE
84 SWAZILAND
85 LESOTHO
86 MAURITIUS
87 UNITED ARAB EMIRATES
88 QATAR
89 BAHRAIN
90 BHUTAN
91 BANGLADESH
92 CAMBODIA

These Pacific island nations can be found on pages 44 and 45.

FEDERAL STATES OF MICRONESIA

FIJI

KIRIBATI

MARSHALL ISLANDS

NAURU

PALAU

TONGA

TUVALU

VANUATU

WESTERN SAMOA

FINLAND

RUSSIAN FEDERATION

ARUS

AINE

46

MACEDONIA

KAZAKHSTAN

MONGOLIA

NORTH KOREA

UZBEKISTAN

55

51
REECE TURKEY 52 53 TURKMENISTAN 54
57
56 59
58 60 IRAQ IRAN AFGHANISTAN
61
89 88
87 PAKISTAN

CHINA

SOUTH KOREA

JAPAN

TAIWAN

NEPAL 90

91

EGYPT

SAUDI ARABIA

OMAN

INDIA

MYANMAR

LAOS
THAILAND
92 VIETNAM

PHILIPPINES

ERITREA

YEMEN

SUDAN

80

SRI LANKA

BRUNEI

MALAYSIA

SINGAPORE

ETHIOPIA

77 KENYA SOMALIA

OCRATIC
PUBLIC
CONGO 78
79

TANZANIA

INDONESIA

PAPUA NEW GUINEA

SOLOMON ISLANDS

ZAMBIA 82

81

MOZAMBIQUE

MADAGASCAR

83

OTSWANA

86

84

85

TH

CA

AUSTRALIA

NEW CALEDONIA

NEW ZEALAND

British Isles

There are two countries in the British Isles – the United Kingdom and the Republic of Ireland. Scotland, England, Wales and Northern Ireland are all part of the United Kingdom. The Isle of Man and the Channel Islands are British Crown Dependencies.

ATLANTIC OCEAN

Shetland pony

Shetland Islands

Oil and gas found under the North Sea bring a lot of money to the United Kingdom.

North Sea

Oxford University
Oxford University set up over 800 years ago and is the oldest university in the British Isles.

Orkney Islands

Electricity is made from nuclear power in some parts of the British Isles.

Many people think they have seen a monster in Loch Ness.

Puffin

Aberdeen

SCOTLAND

Ben Nevis (1343m)

NORTH WEST HIGHLANDS

GRAMPIAN MOUNTAINS

Edinburgh

Wildcat
A few wildcats as well as the rare Golden Eagle still live in the Scottish Highlands.

Glasgow

Golden eagle

U N I T E D

H E B R I D E S

Emerald Isle
Many people visit the beautiful green countryside of Ireland which is often called the Emerald Isle.

NORTHERN IRELAND

The Humber Bridge is one of the longest bridges in the world.

The Channel tunnel between England and France is nearly 50 kilometres long.

Newcastle upon Tyne

Hull

ENGLAND

Fox

Cambridge

Big Ben

Sheffield

Leeds

Bradford

LONDON

Leicester

Manchester

Nottingham

Coventry

Birmingham

Badger

Oxford

Portsmouth

PENNINES

Hadrian's

LAKE DISTRICT

R. Thames

Southampton

K I N G D O M

R. Severn

R. COTSWOLDS

Bristol

Stonehenge

English Channel

Liverpool

CAMBRIAN MOUNTAINS

Cardiff

DARTMOOR

Plymouth

Isle of Man

Conwy

Snowdon (1085m)

WALES

Channel Is.

Irish Sea

Belfast

DUBLIN

WICKLOW MOUNTAINS

REPUBLIC OF IRELAND

R. Shannon

Cork

Celtic Sea

Conwy Castle in Wales is Conwy Castle in one of many castles in the British Isles.

Racehorses are bred in Ireland

N E S W

13

Northern Europe

There are five countries in Northern Europe: Iceland, Norway, Sweden, Denmark and Finland. Three of the countries, Norway, Sweden and Denmark, are known as Scandinavia. Iceland is an island in the North Atlantic, a long distance from the rest of Europe.

Midnight skiing
Inside the Arctic Circle the sun hardly sets at all in the summer. These people are skiing at midnight in Lapland.

Lapps
The Lapp people are reindeer farmers who live in the far north of Norway, Sweden, Finland and the former U.S.S.R.

Hammerfest is the most northerly town in the world.

Lapp with reindeer

ARCTIC CIRCLE

Ptarmigan

Arctic fox

Oulu

Gulf of Bothnia

Hammerfest

Narvik

Bodø

NORWAY

ATLANTIC OCEAN

Fjord
The coast of Norway is cut by lots of steep-sided inlets called fjords.

ICELAND

Puffins

Geyser

REYKJAVÍK

R. Thjórsá

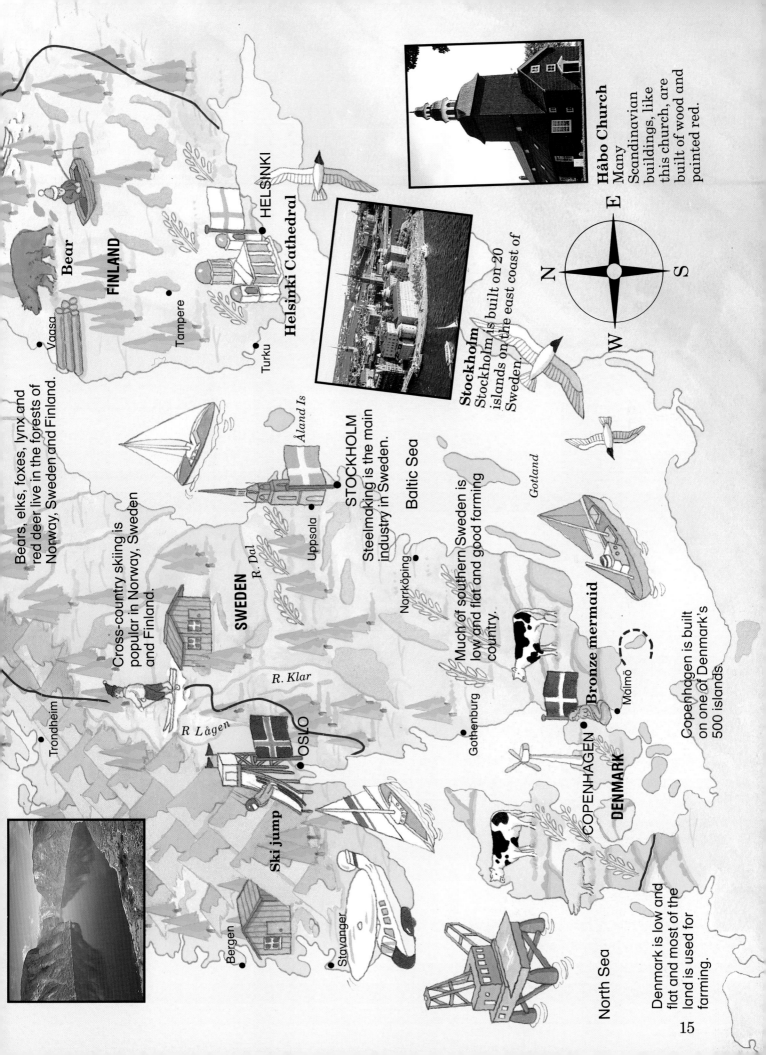

Håbo Church Many Scandinavian buildings, like this church, are built of wood and painted red.

Bear

FINLAND

Vaasa

Tampere

Turku

HELSINKI

Helsinki Cathedral

Bears, elks, foxes, lynx and red deer live in the forests of Norway, Sweden and Finland.

Stockholm Stockholm is built on 20 islands on the east coast of Sweden.

N
W E
S

Åland Is

R. Dal

Cross-country skiing is popular in Norway, Sweden and Finland.

SWEDEN

Uppsala

STOCKHOLM Steelmaking is the main industry in Sweden.

Baltic Sea

Gotland

Norrköping

Much of southern Sweden is low and flat and good farming country.

R. Klar

Trondheim

R Lågen

OSLO

Ski jump

Bergen

Stavanger

Gothenburg

Malmö

COPENHAGEN

Bronze mermaid

DENMARK

Copenhagen is built on one of Denmark's 500 islands.

North Sea

Denmark is low and flat and most of the land is used for farming.

15

Western and Central Europe

These regions stretch from the Atlantic Ocean in the west to Black Sea in the east. Most low land is used for farming, but there are still large forests where wild animals live.

North Sea

THE NETHERLANDS

Hamburg •

• Amsterdam
THE HAGUE

Rotterdam •

GERMANY

Eiffel Tower

Antwerp •

Leipzig

R. Seine

BRUSSELS
BELGIUM

Bonn •

LUXEMBOURG

R. Rhine

Frankfurt •

PARIS •

The T.G.V. is the fastest train in the world.

Strasbourg •

Industry is very advanced in Germany and cars as well as other goods are sold all over the world.

More than 300 different kinds of cheese are made in France.

R. Loire

FRANCE

Zürich •

Munich •

Loire château

ATLANTIC OCEAN

Lyon •

BERN •

LIECHTENSTEIN

A

Geneva •

SWITZERLAND

Bordeaux •

Mt. Blanc (4807m)

R. Rhône

Toulouse •

Oil refinery

PYRENEES

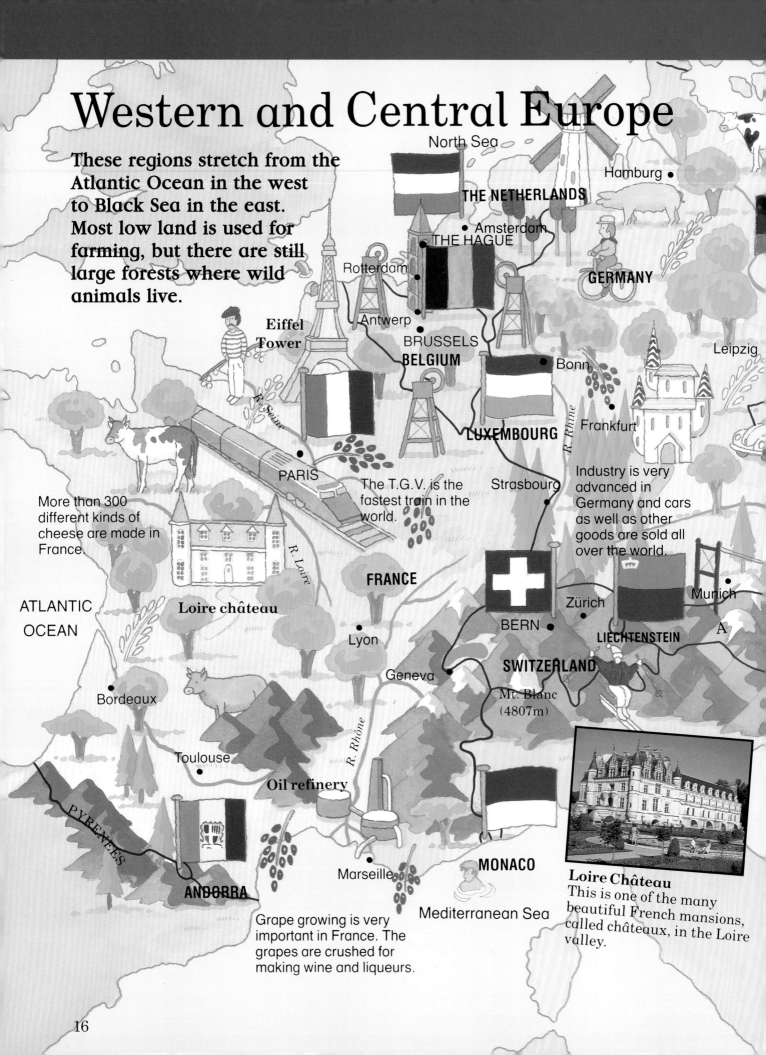

MONACO

Loire Château
This is one of the many beautiful French mansions, called châteaux, in the Loire valley.

ANDORRA

Marseille •

Mediterranean Sea

Grape growing is very important in France. The grapes are crushed for making wine and liqueurs.

Baltic Sea

Ship building yard
Gdańsk •

European Bison

BERLIN •

R. Oder

Dresden

POLAND   WARSAW •

R. Vistula

Rose plantation
Fields of roses are grown in Bulgaria. The petals are used for making perfume.

PRAGUE •

CZECH REPUBLIC

Cracow •

CARPATHIAN MOUNTAINS

SLOVAKIA

VIENNA • • BRATISLAVA

Budapest is really two towns, Buda and Pest, which are separated by the River Danube.

P   S

AUSTRIA

• BUDAPEST

HUNGARY

ROMANIA

TRANSYLVANIAN ALPS

R. Danube

BUCHAREST •

Chamois
(pronounced *shamwa*)
Chamois live high in the mountain crags in summer, but move down to the forests in winter.

Wolves and bears live in the mountains.

N

W   E

S

SOFIA •

BALKAN MOUNTAINS

BULGARIA

17

The Mediterranean

The Mediterranean Sea lies between Europe and Africa. The countries next to it have hot, dry summers and it is a very popular place for summer holidays.

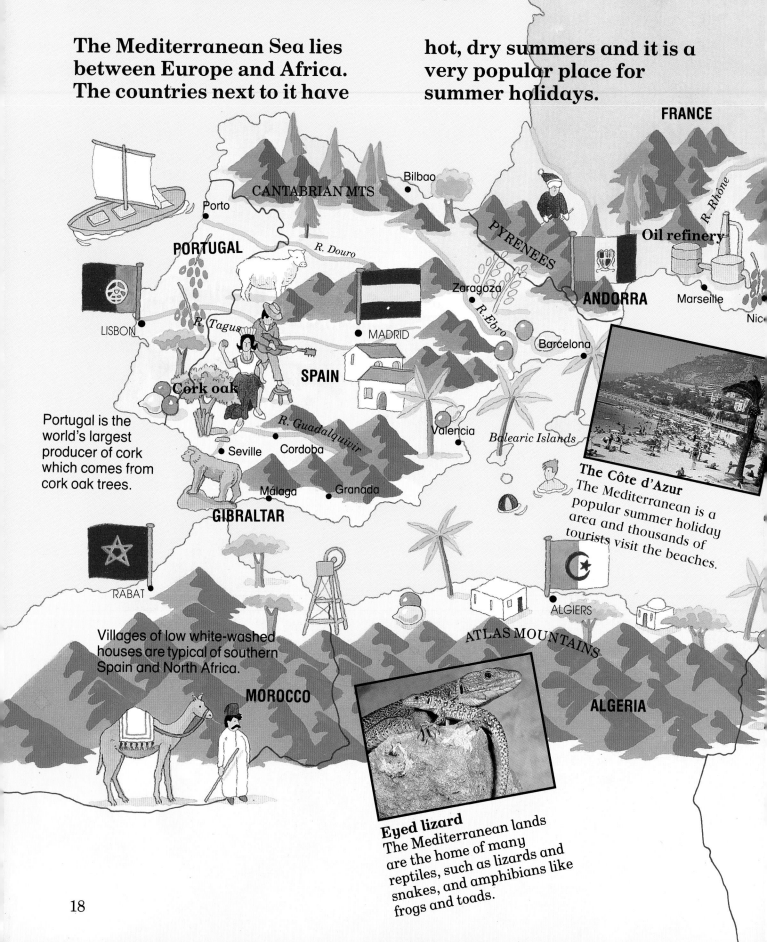

FRANCE

CANTABRIAN MTS

Bilbao

Porto

PORTUGAL

R. Douro

PYRENEES

R. Rhône

Oil refinery

Zaragoza

ANDORRA

R. Ebro

Marseille

MADRID

Barcelona

Nic

R. Tagus

LISBON

SPAIN

Cork oak

Valencia

Balearic Islands

Portugal is the world's largest producer of cork which comes from cork oak trees.

R. Guadalquivir

Seville

Cordoba

Málaga

Granada

The Côte d'Azur
The Mediterranean is a popular summer holiday area and thousands of tourists visit the beaches.

GIBRALTAR

RABAT

Villages of low white-washed houses are typical of southern Spain and North Africa.

ALGIERS

ATLAS MOUNTAINS

MOROCCO

ALGERIA

Eyed lizard
The Mediterranean lands are the home of many reptiles, such as lizards and snakes, and amphibians like frogs and toads.

N
W E
S

ALPS

DOLOMITES

LJUBLJANA

SLOVENIA

Milan

rin

Trieste

Venice

R Po

**Leaning Tower
of Pisa**

ZAGREB

CROATIA

Novi Sad

NACO

APENNINES

Florence

Pisa

SAN MARINO

BOSNIA
HERZEGOVINA

SARAJEVO

BELGRADE

ITALY

Adriatic Sea

orsica

ROME

VATICAN CITY

YUGOSLAVIA

Mt Vesuvius
(1277m)

SKOPJE

dinia

MACEDONIA

liari

Bari

TIRANA

ALBANIA

PINDUS
MOUNTAINS

Naples

Mediterranean Sea

GREECE

Aegean Sea

Mt Etna
(3340m)

Palermo

ATHENS

Sicily

Catania

JNIS

NISIA

MALTA

Crete

In 1991, the country of
Yugoslavia broke up and
the region now has five
independent nations.
These are called Slovenia,
Croatia, Bosnia-Herzegovina,
Yugoslavia and Macedonia.

Holy monastery
This is one of a
group of Greek
monasteries built
on rock pillars.

Vatican City
Vatican City, in the west of
Rome, is the world's smallest
country and is ruled by the
Pope.

19

Russia and its Borders

In 1991, the U.S.S.R. (Union of Soviet Socialist Republics) broke up into 15 independent states, of which the Russian Federation is the largest. Most of these countries belong to the Commonwealth of Independent States.

St. Basil's Cathedral
St. Basil's Cathedral is next to the Red Square in the centre of Moscow. It was built 400 years ago.

ARCTIC OCEAN

Walrus

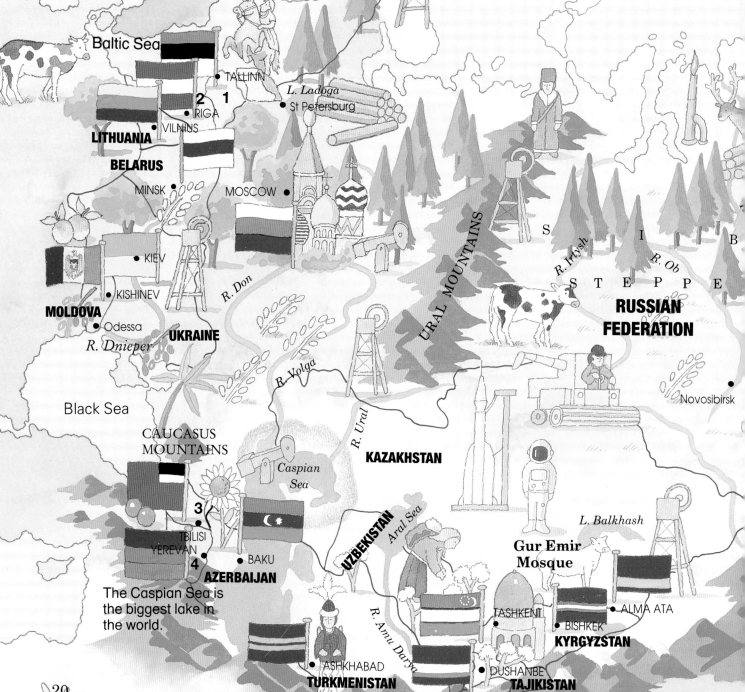

Baltic Sea

TALLINN

2 **1**

L. Ladoga

RIGA

St Petersburg

VILNIUS

LITHUANIA

BELARUS

MINSK

MOSCOW

KIEV

R. Don

KISHINEV

R. Volga

MOLDOVA

Odessa

R. Dnieper

UKRAINE

Black Sea

CAUCASUS MOUNTAINS

Caspian Sea

3

TBILISI

YEREVAN

4

BAKU

AZERBAIJAN

The Caspian Sea is the biggest lake in the world.

R. Ural

KAZAKHSTAN

URAL MOUNTAINS

S I B

R. Irtysh

R. Ob

S T E P P E

RUSSIAN FEDERATION

Novosibirsk

L. Balkhash

Gur Emir Mosque

Aral Sea

UZBEKISTAN

TASHKENT

ALMA ATA

BISHKEK

KYRGYZSTAN

R. Amu Darya

ASHKHABAD

DUSHANBE

TURKMENISTAN **TAJIKISTAN**

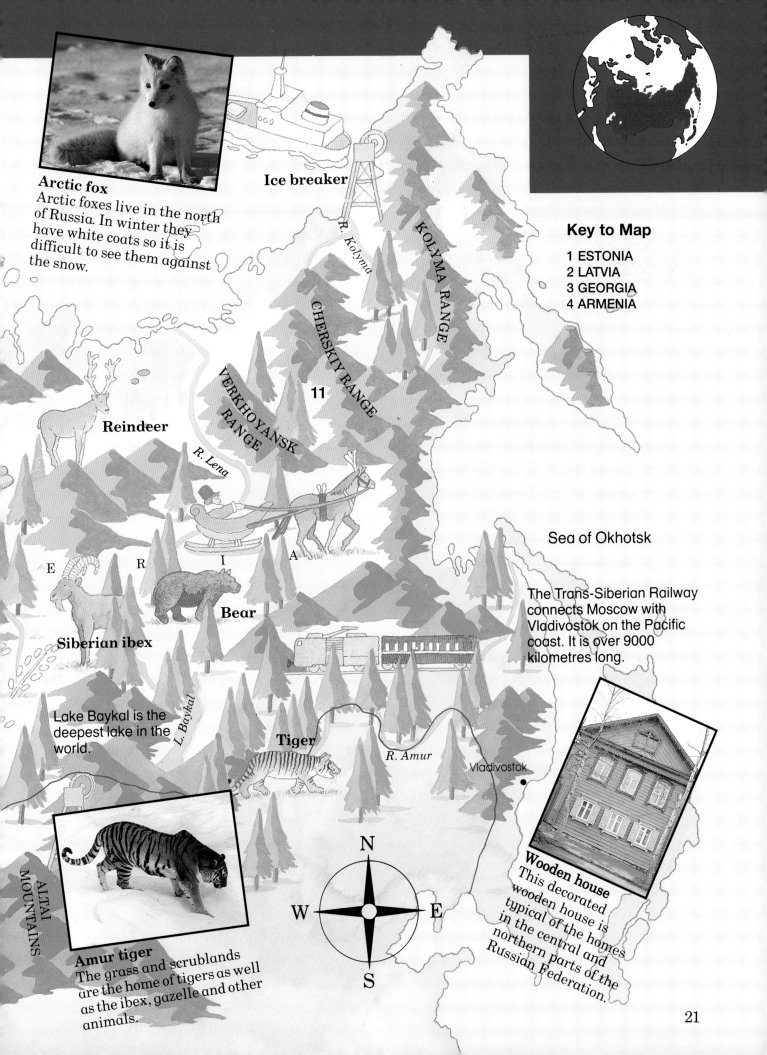

Arctic fox
Arctic foxes live in the north of Russia. In winter they have white coats so it is difficult to see them against the snow.

Ice breaker

R. Kolyma

KOLYMA RANGE

CHERSKIY RANGE

VERKHOYANSK RANGE

11

Key to Map

1 ESTONIA
2 LATVIA
3 GEORGIA
4 ARMENIA

Reindeer

R. Lena

E   R   I   A

Bear

Siberian ibex

Lake Baykal is the deepest lake in the world.

L. Baykal

Tiger

R. Amur

Sea of Okhotsk

The Trans-Siberian Railway connects Moscow with Vladivostok on the Pacific coast. It is over 9000 kilometres long.

Vladivostok

Wooden house
This decorated wooden house is typical of the homes in the central and northern parts of the Russian Federation.

ALTAI MOUNTAINS

Amur tiger
The grass and scrublands are the home of tigers as well as the ibex, gazelle and other animals.

N
W   E
S

21

North America

North America includes two very large countries – Canada, which is the largest country in the world, and the United States of America (the U.S.A.). The U.S.A. is made up of 50 states; 48 are in the southern half of the continent but Alaska is in the far north west and the Hawaiian Islands – the 50th state – are in the Pacific Ocean.

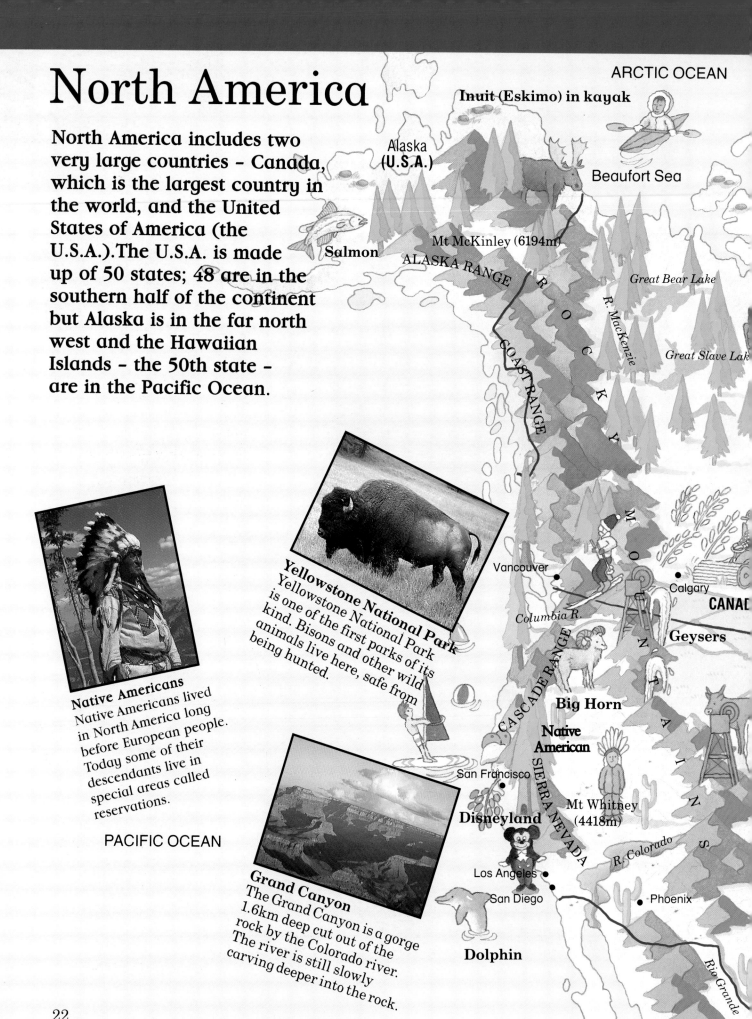

ARCTIC OCEAN

Inuit (Eskimo) in kayak

Alaska (U.S.A.)

Beaufort Sea

Salmon

Mt McKinley (6194m)

ALASKA RANGE

ROCKY

COAST RANGE

Great Bear Lake

R. MacKenzie

Great Slave Lake

Vancouver

Columbia R.

Calgary

CANAD

MOUNTAINS

Geysers

CASCADE RANGE

Big Horn

Native American

San Francisco

Disneyland

SIERRA NEVADA

Mt Whitney (4418m)

Los Angeles

R. Colorado

San Diego

Phoenix

Dolphin

Rio Grande

PACIFIC OCEAN

Native Americans
Native Americans lived in North America long before European people. Today some of their descendants live in special areas called reservations.

Yellowstone National Park
Yellowstone National Park is one of the first parks of its kind. Bisons and other wild animals live here, safe from being hunted.

Grand Canyon
The Grand Canyon is a gorge 1.6km deep cut out of the rock by the Colorado river. The river is still slowly carving deeper into the rock.

Greenland

Polar bear

Igloo

N

W E

S

Labrador Sea

Arctic fox

Narwhal

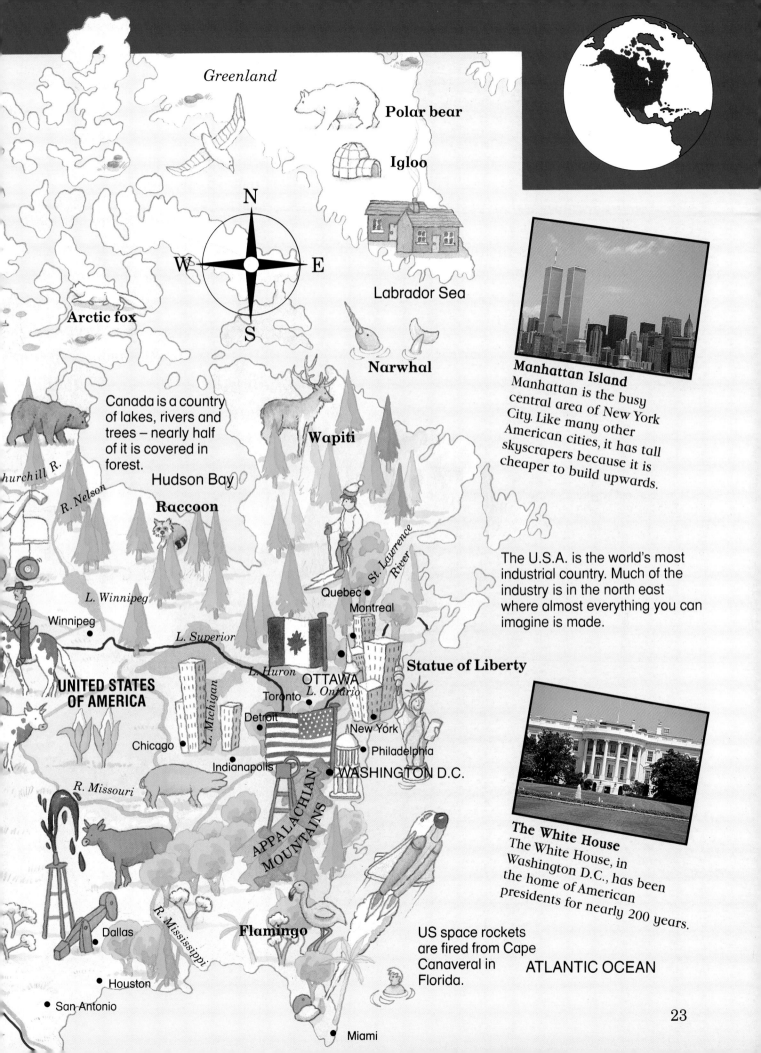

Manhattan Island
Manhattan is the busy central area of New York City. Like many other American cities, it has tall skyscrapers because it is cheaper to build upwards.

Canada is a country of lakes, rivers and trees – nearly half of it is covered in forest. Hudson Bay

Wapiti

Raccoon

Churchill R.

R. Nelson

L. Winnipeg

Winnipeg

The U.S.A. is the world's most industrial country. Much of the industry is in the north east where almost everything you can imagine is made.

St. Lawrence River

Quebec

Montreal

L. Superior

L. Huron

OTTAWA

Toronto

L. Ontario

Statue of Liberty

UNITED STATES OF AMERICA

L. Michigan

Detroit

New York

Chicago

Philadelphia

Indianapolis

WASHINGTON D.C.

R. Missouri

APPALACHIAN MOUNTAINS

The White House
The White House, in Washington D.C., has been the home of American presidents for nearly 200 years.

R. Mississippi

Flamingo

Dallas

US space rockets are fired from Cape Canaveral in Florida.

ATLANTIC OCEAN

Houston

San Antonio

Miami

Central America and Caribbean

Central America is a hot, mountainous land link between the North and South **American continents. To the east, across the Caribbean Sea, are thousands of tropical islands.**

EASTERN SIERRA MADRE

WESTERN SIERRA MADRE

Gulf Of California

Mayan Temple
This temple was built over 3000 years ago by the Mayan people who lived in southern Mexico and Guatemala.

Flying fish

Gulf of Mexico

Valuable woods, such as mahogany and rosewood, grow in the tropical forests.

Mexico produces more silver than anywhere else in the world as well as huge amounts of oil.

Popocatépetl (5452m)

MEXICO CITY

MEXICO

Tapir

BELMOPAN

BELIZE

HONDURAS

GUATEMALA

GUATEMALA CITY

EL SALVADOR

SAN SALVADOR

MANAGUA

NICARAGUA

Silky Anteater
Anteaters are common in the tropical rainforests.

Swordfish

COSTA RICA

Hummingbird
The tiny hummingbird lives in the tropical rainforests. It beats its wings very fast to hover and drink the nectar of tropical flowers.

Dolphin

PACIFIC OCEAN

Bananas
These people are picking bananas. Many of the small countries in Central America rely mainly on growing bananas, coffee and sugar cane for their wealth.

Bermuda

ATLANTIC OCEAN

Caribbean Islands
Almost all of the Caribbean islands have sandy beaches and warm, sunny weather most of the year round. People come to sail, swim and snorkel in the warm sea and relax on the beaches.

BAHAMAS

● HAVANA

CUBA

Cayman Islands

Turks & Caicos Islands

DOMINICAN REPUBLIC

HAITI

JAMAICA
KINGSTON ●

Greater Antilles

PORT-AU-PRINCE

SANTO DOMINGO

SAN JUAN

PUERTO RICO

VIRGIN ISLANDS

ST. KITTS – NEVIS

ANTIGUA & BARBUDA

GUADELOUPE

DOMINICA

MARTINIQUE

ST. LUCIA

ST. VINCENT

GRENADA

BARBADOS

TRINIDAD & TOBAGO

Lesser Antilles

Caribbean Sea

Large turtles are found in the warm southern seas.

Toucan

Parrot

SAN JOSE

Panama Canal

PANAMA CITY

PANAMA

Hurricanes
There are sometimes violent storms, called hurricanes, in Central America and the Caribbean. These hurricanes bring very strong winds, heavy rain and large sea waves which can cause a lot of damage.

N
W   E
S

25

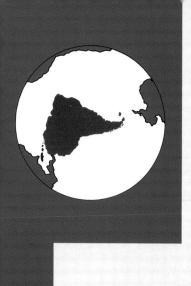

South America

There are 13 countries in South America. In the north of the continent it is very hot, with the huge tropical Amazon forest and the

Amazon river which is in volume the biggest river on earth. The southern tip of South America is close to the Antarctic and is very cold.

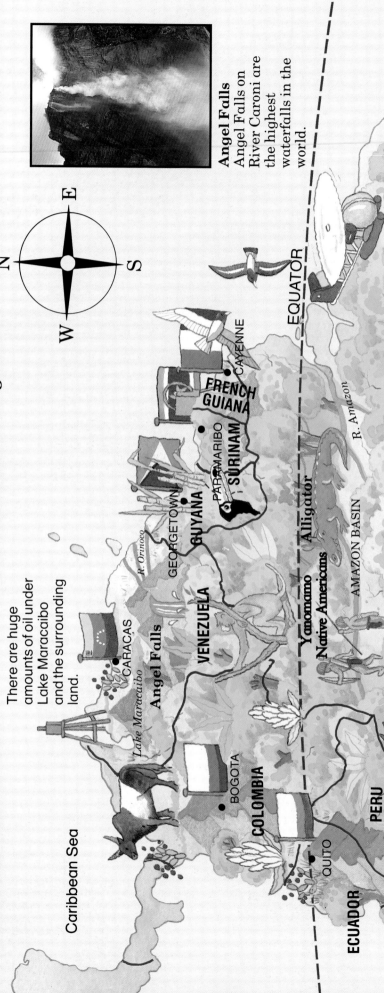

Angel Falls
Angel Falls on River Caroni are the highest waterfalls in the world.

ATLANTIC OCEAN

N
E
S
W

There are huge amounts of oil under Lake Maracaibo and the surrounding land.

Caribbean Sea

CARACAS
Lake Maracaibo
Angel Falls
VENEZUELA

BOGOTA
COLOMBIA

R. Orinoco
GEORGETOWN
GUYANA
PARAMARIBO
SURINAM
CAYENNE
FRENCH GUIANA

QUITO
ECUADOR

PERU
Condor

Yanomamo
Native Americans
Alligator

AMAZON BASIN
R. Amazon

EQUATOR

Toucan

BRAZIL
Jaguar

Parakeet

Statue of Christ on Corcovado Peak

Cocoa

BRASILIA

Rio de Janeiro

São Paulo

Every February there is a colourful carnival in Rio de Janeiro.

R. Paraná

The Yanomamo
The Yanomamo, such as Native Americans, clear an the Yanomamo, for their area of the forest. They also villages and crops. They also hunt and fish with spears or a bow and arrow.

Llamas
Llamas are farmed in the Andes. Native American people make warm clothes from their wool.

BOLIVIA

LA PAZ

S

E

CHILE

PARAGUAY

ASUNCION

ARGENTINA
South American cowboy

URUGUAY

MONTEVIDEO

BUENOS AIRES

PAMPAS

The Pampas is a huge area of rich grasslands where millions of sheep and cattle graze.

Whale

ATACAMA

The Atacama Desert is one of the driest places in the world.

SANTIAGO

A N D E S

PATAGONIAN DESERT

There are many earthquakes in Chile.

Falkland Is.

Tierra del Fuego

Ushuaia

Ushuaia is the most southerly town in the world.

PACIFIC OCEAN

Fishing is important off the coast of Ecuador and Peru.

Lake Titicaca
Lake Titicaca is the highest large lake in the world at 3811m above the sea. The Native Americans fish in boats made from reeds which grow around the lake.

Marmoset
Marmosets and many other wild animals live in the Amazon Basin, which has the biggest forest in the world.

Africa

Africa is the second largest continent of the world and it is split up into lots of countries. There are large deserts, grasslands and tropical forests with many different kinds of animals and groups of people living in them.

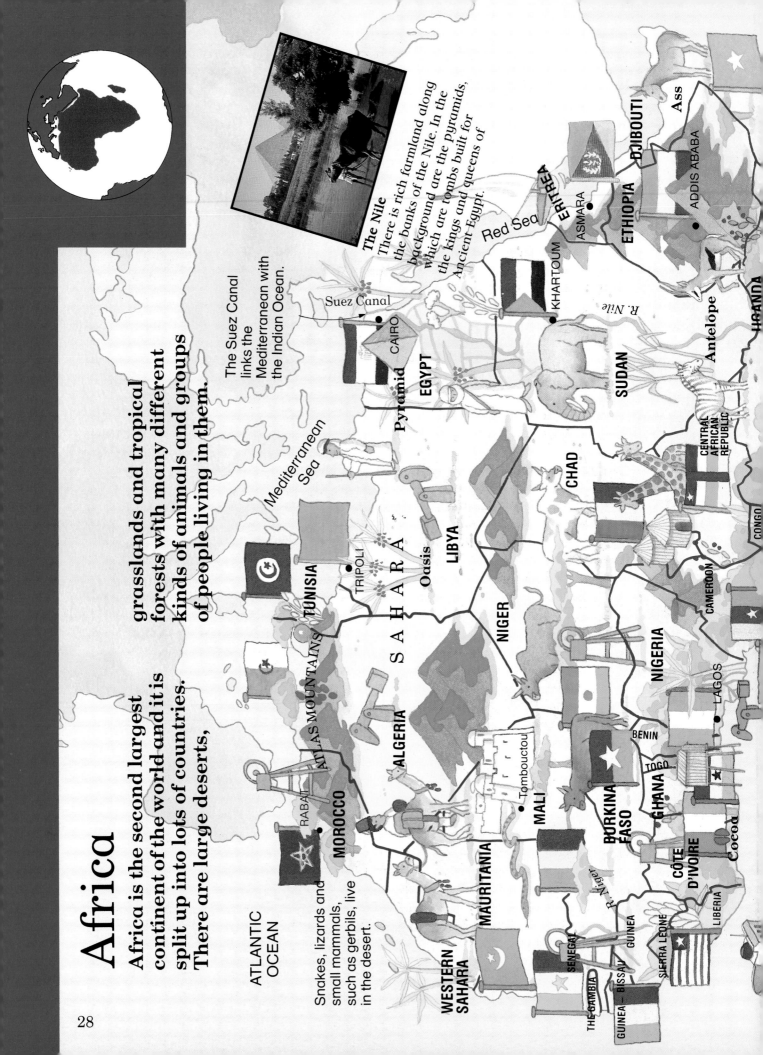

The Suez Canal links the Mediterranean with the Indian Ocean.

The Nile
There is rich farmland along the banks of the Nile. In the background are the Pyramids, which are tombs built for the kings and queens of Ancient Egypt.

Snakes, lizards and small mammals, such as gerbils, live in the desert.

ATLANTIC OCEAN

Mediterranean Sea

Suez Canal

Red Sea

R. Nile

R. Niger

SAHARA

Oasis

Pyramid

ATLAS MOUNTAINS

RABAT

MOROCCO

WESTERN SAHARA

MAURITANIA

TUNISIA

TRIPOLI

ALGERIA

LIBYA

EGYPT

CAIRO

KHARTOUM

SUDAN

ERITREA

ASMARA

DJIBOUTI

ETHIOPIA

ADDIS ABABA

Ass

Antelope

UGANDA

CHAD

NIGER

CENTRAL AFRICAN REPUBLIC

CAMEROON

CONGO

NIGERIA

LAGOS

BENIN

TOGO

GHANA

Cocoa

BURKINA FASO

CÔTE D'IVOIRE

LIBERIA

SIERRA LEONE

GUINEA

GUINEA-BISSAU

THE GAMBIA

SENEGAL

MALI

Tombouctou

28

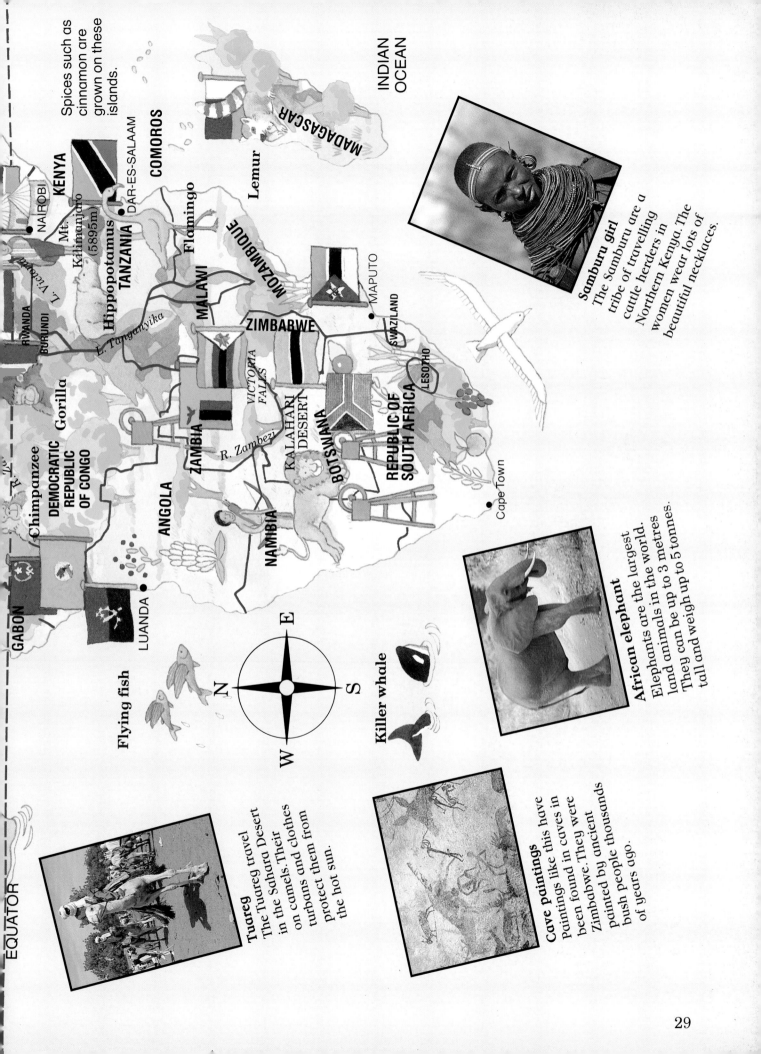

Spices such as cinnamon are grown on these islands.

INDIAN OCEAN

KENYA

Mt. Kilimanjaro (5895m)

NAIROBI

DAR-ES-SALAAM

COMOROS

MADAGASCAR

Lemur

Hippopotamus TANZANIA

L. Victoria

RWANDA

BURUNDI

L. Tanganyika

Flamingo

MALAWI

MOZAMBIQUE

MAPUTO

Gorilla

Chimpanzee

DEMOCRATIC REPUBLIC OF CONGO

ZIMBABWE

SWAZILAND

VICTORIA FALLS

LESOTHO

KALAHARI DESERT

ANGOLA

ZAMBIA

BOTSWANA

REPUBLIC OF SOUTH AFRICA

R. Zambezi

NAMIBIA

GABON

LUANDA

Cape Town

Flying fish

N E S W

Killer whale

Samburu girl
The Samburu are a tribe of travelling cattle herders in Northern Kenya. The women wear lots of beautiful necklaces.

African elephant
African elephants are the largest land animals in the world. Elephants are up to 3 metres tall and weigh up to 5 tonnes.

Tuareg
The Tuareg travel the Sahara Desert on camels. Their clothes and turbans protect them from the hot sun.

Cave paintings
Paintings like this have been found in caves in Zimbabwe. They were painted by ancient bush people thousands of years ago.

29

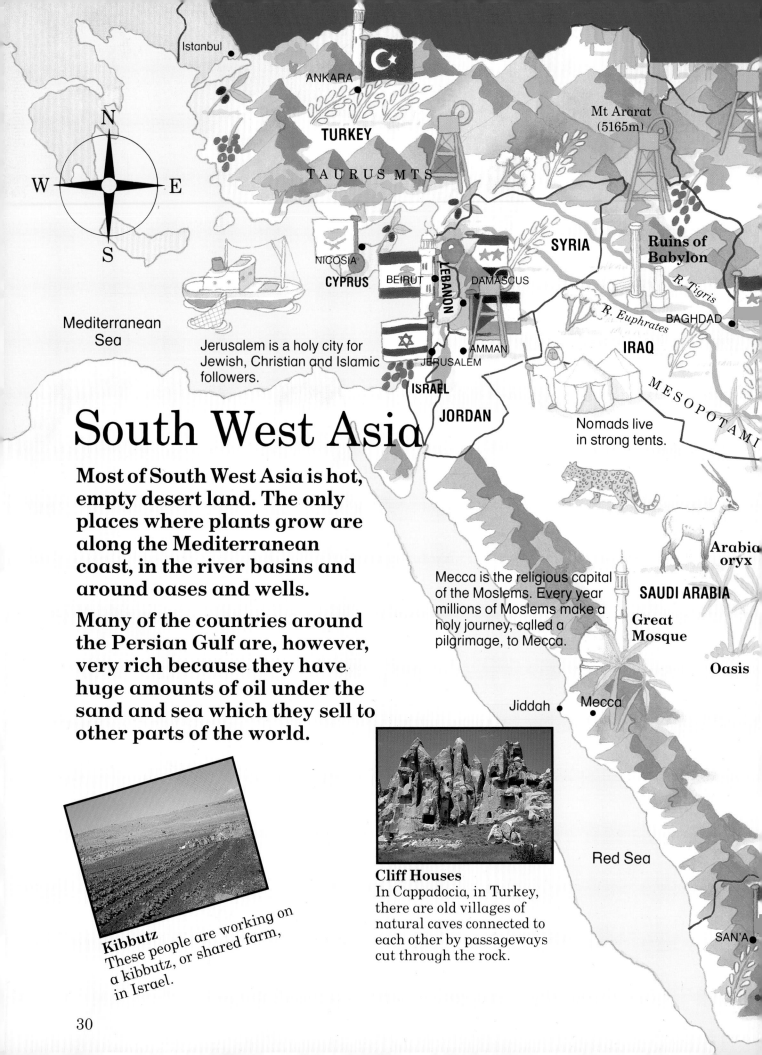

Istanbul

ANKARA

TURKEY

Mt Ararat
(5165m)

T A U R U S   M T S

SYRIA

Ruins of Babylon

NICOSIA

BEIRUT

LEBANON

DAMASCUS

R. Tigris

CYPRUS

R. Euphrates

BAGHDAD

Mediterranean
Sea

Jerusalem is a holy city for
Jewish, Christian and Islamic
followers.

AMMAN

JERUSALEM

IRAQ

M E S O P O T A M I

ISRAEL

JORDAN

Nomads live
in strong tents.

South West Asia

**Most of South West Asia is hot,
empty desert land. The only
places where plants grow are
along the Mediterranean
coast, in the river basins and
around oases and wells.**

**Many of the countries around
the Persian Gulf are, however,
very rich because they have
huge amounts of oil under the
sand and sea which they sell to
other parts of the world.**

Arabia
oryx

Mecca is the religious capital
of the Moslems. Every year
millions of Moslems make a
holy journey, called a
pilgrimage, to Mecca.

SAUDI ARABIA

**Great
Mosque**

Oasis

Jiddah   Mecca

Kibbutz
These people are working on
a kibbutz, or shared farm,
in Israel.

Cliff Houses
In Cappadocia, in Turkey,
there are old villages of
natural caves connected to
each other by passageways
cut through the rock.

Red Sea

SAN'A

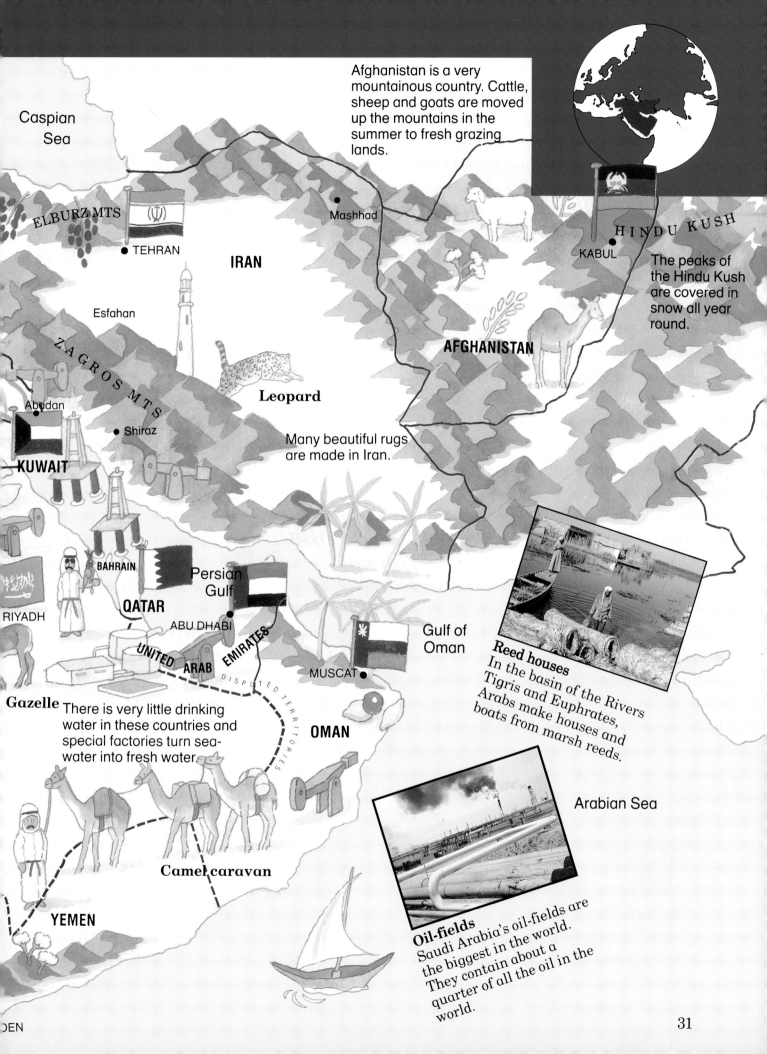

Caspian Sea

Afghanistan is a very mountainous country. Cattle, sheep and goats are moved up the mountains in the summer to fresh grazing lands.

ELBURZ MTS

Mashhad

• TEHRAN

IRAN

HINDU KUSH

KABUL

The peaks of the Hindu Kush are covered in snow all year round.

Esfahan

ZAGROS MTS

Abadan

• Shiraz

AFGHANISTAN

Leopard

Many beautiful rugs are made in Iran.

KUWAIT

BAHRAIN

Persian Gulf

QATAR

RIYADH

ABU DHABI

UNITED ARAB EMIRATES

DISPUTED TERRITORIES

MUSCAT •

Gulf of Oman

Reed houses
In the basin of the Rivers Tigris and Euphrates, Arabs make houses and boats from marsh reeds.

OMAN

Gazelle There is very little drinking water in these countries and special factories turn sea-water into fresh water.

Arabian Sea

Camel caravan

YEMEN

Oil-fields
Saudi Arabia's oil-fields are the biggest in the world. They contain about a quarter of all the oil in the world.

DEN

South Asia

South Asia includes India, Pakistan, Bangladesh, Nepal and Bhutan as well as Sri Lanka and the Maldive islands. The area is separated from the rest of Asia by the Himalayas – the highest mountain range in the world. South Asia is a farming area and the crops depend on monsoon rains which fall between June and October. The rain is badly needed at the end of a long, hot, dry season and there is great hardship if it arrives late.

Flooding
Flooding is common in Bangladesh in the rainy season. The rivers flood and often destroy homes and crops.

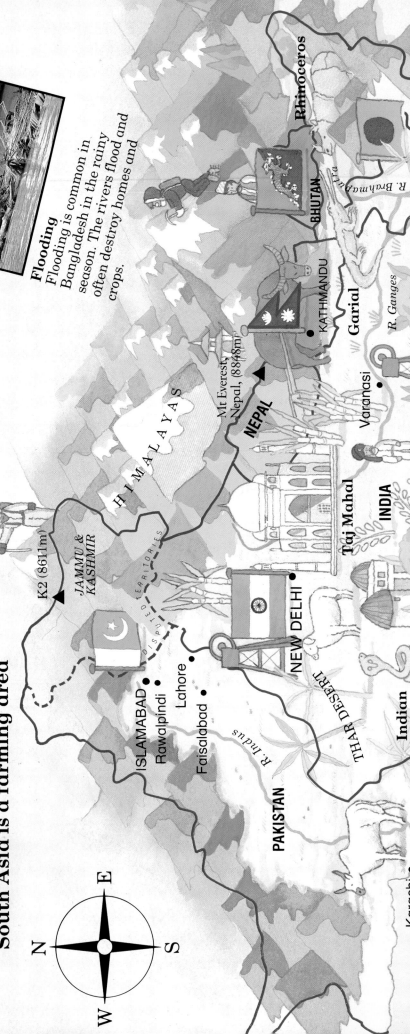

Rhinoceros

BHUTAN

R. Brahmaputra

DHAKA

KATHMANDU

Garial

R. Ganges

HIMALAYAS

Mt Everest, Nepal, (8848m)

NEPAL

Varanasi

K2 (8611m)

JAMMU & KASHMIR

DISPUTED TERRITORIES

Taj Mahal

INDIA

NEW DELHI

ISLAMABAD
Rawalpindi
Lahore
Faisalabad

R. Indus

THAR DESERT

Indian cobra

PAKISTAN

Karachi

N
E
S
W

Calcutta

BANGLADESH

Andaman Is.

Nicobar Is.

Ganges river
The Ganges is holy to Hindus and about a million people visit Varanasi every year to bathe in the river.

R. Mahanadi

Flying fish

Bay of Bengal

R. Godavari

DECCAN PLATEAU

• Hyderabad

R. Krishna

• Madras

Sacred cow
Cows wander about freely in India, even in the cities. Hindus believe that cows are holy and must not be harmed.

Elephant

SRI LANKA

COLOMBO •

INDIAN OCEAN

R. Narmada

Bangalore

• Bombay

Goa •

Arabian Sea

Ahmadabad

Lakshadweep

MALDIVES

The Maldives are a country made up of 2000 coral islands. People only live on 220 of the islands.

Street traders
Streets in India are often crowded with traders selling fruit and vegetables from the country as well as other goods.

Tea plantation
More tea is grown in India than anywhere else in the world. This woman is plucking the tea-leaves.

South East Asia

South East Asia is a hot, wet, tropical area. It is made up of Myanmar, Thailand, Malaysia, Singapore, Laos, Vietnam, Cambodia, Brunei, Papua New Guinea and the thousands of islands of Indonesia and the Philippines.

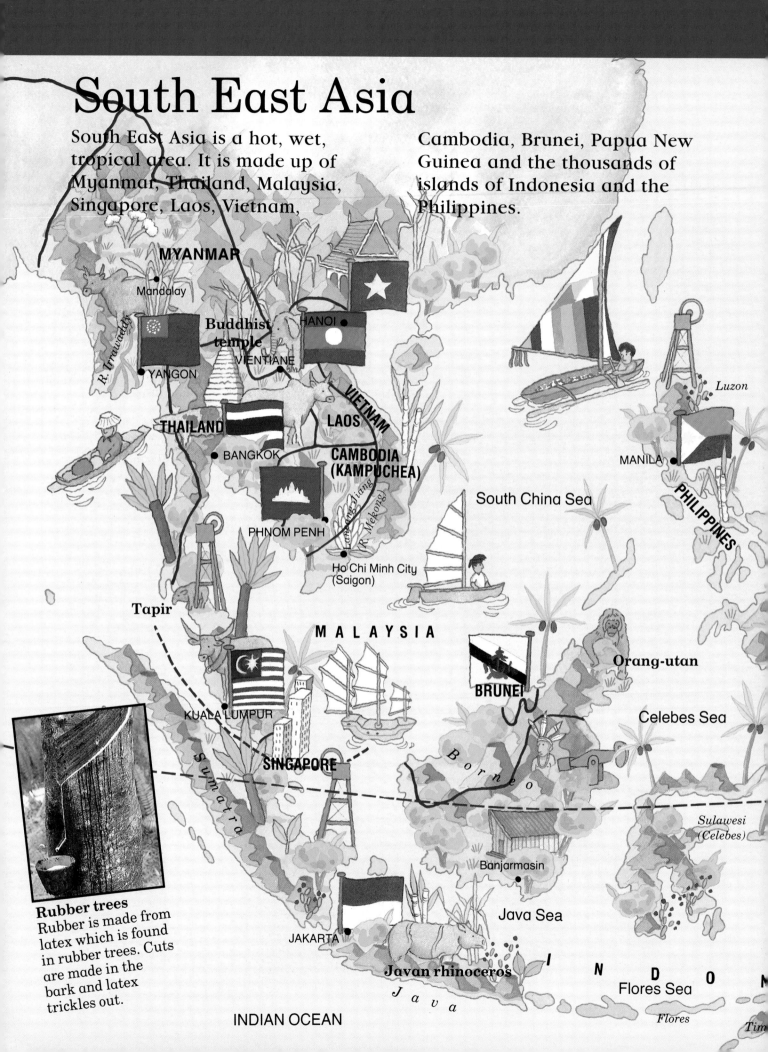

MYANMAR

Mandalay

R. Irrawaddy

Buddhist temple

HANOI

VIENTIANE

YANGON

THAILAND

BANGKOK

LAOS

VIETNAM

CAMBODIA (KAMPUCHEA)

PHNOM PENH

Lancang Jiang (R. Mekong)

Ho Chi Minh City (Saigon)

South China Sea

Luzon

MANILA

PHILIPPINES

Tapir

MALAYSIA

Orang-utan

BRUNEI

Celebes Sea

Borneo

KUALA LUMPUR

Sumatra

SINGAPORE

Sulawesi (Celebes)

Banjarmasin

Java Sea

JAKARTA

Javan rhinoceros

I N D O N

Flores Sea

Java

Flores

INDIAN OCEAN

Tim

Rubber trees
Rubber is made from latex which is found in rubber trees. Cuts are made in the bark and latex trickles out.

Terraces in the Philippines
Where the land is hilly, rice fields are cut like steps into the hillside. These are called terraces.

Floating market
Many people in Bangkok live on boats as the land is very crowded. This is a floating fruit and vegetable market.

Orang-utan
The tropical forests are full of wild animals such as orang-utans, leopards, rhinoceroses, tapirs and tigers.

PACIFIC OCEAN

Mindanao

Village on stilts
Many of the houses along the river valleys in Thailand are on stilts. When the rivers flood, the houses stay above the water.

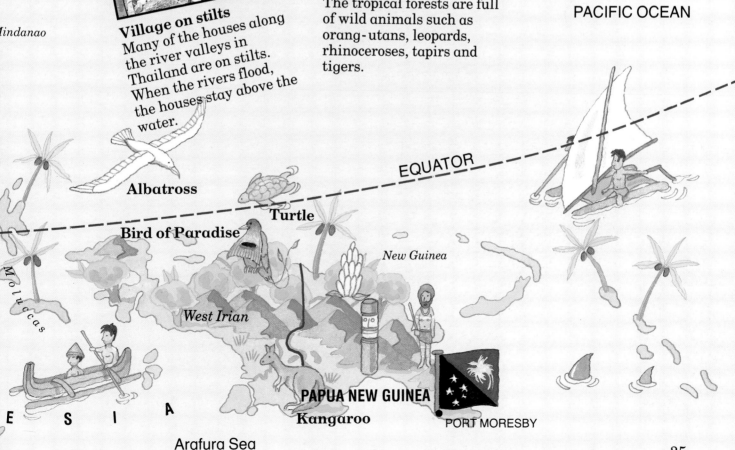

Albatross

Turtle

Bird of Paradise

New Guinea

EQUATOR

Moluccas

West Irian

PAPUA NEW GUINEA

Kangaroo

● PORT MORESBY

E S I A

Arafura Sea

Japan

Japan is made up of four large and about 3000 small islands and is around the same size as the British Isles. Mountains run all the way down the main islands with many old and active volcanoes.

Japan is one of the richest countries in Asia, with many well run factories making goods such as cars, television sets and ships. It is also a very crowded country and people live in small houses or flats which use less space.

Cormorant

People go skiing and ski-jumping in the mountains.

Hokkaidō

Buddha

Black bear

Sapporo

Otter

PACIFIC OCEAN

Sea of Japan

Japanese macaque

Crested ibis

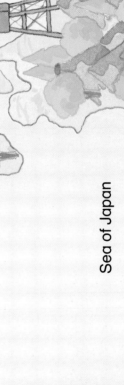

Japanese Macaque
This monkey lives alongside badgers, bears, otters, wolves and other animals in the forests.

There are about 1000 earthquakes every year in Japan but most of them are only small tremors.

The Golden Pavilion
The main religions in Japan are Buddhism and Shinto. These are Buddhist holy temples. People visit holy temples, like this, with gifts of fruit and flowers.

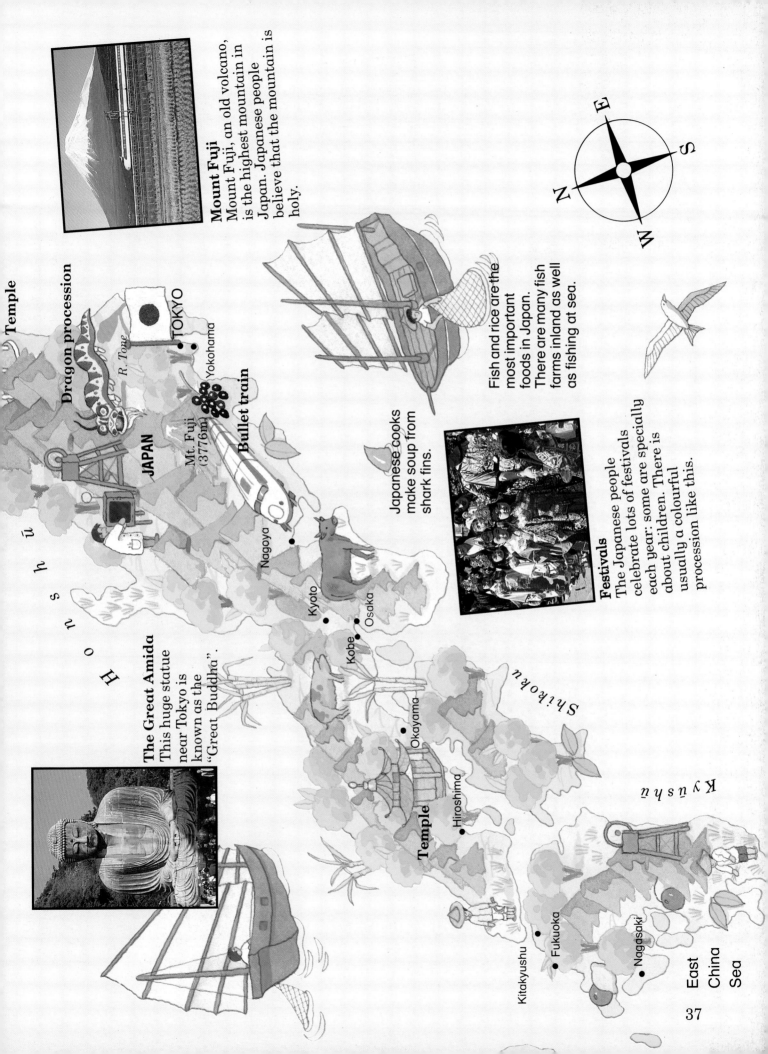

Mount Fuji
Mount Fuji, an old volcano, is the highest mountain in Japan. Japanese people believe that the mountain is holy.

E
N — S
W

Temple

Dragon procession

R. Tone

TOKYO
Yokohama

JAPAN

Mt. Fuji
(3776m)

Bullet train

Nagoya

Kyoto
Osaka
Kobe

H o n s h ū

The Great Amida
This huge statue near Tokyo is known as the "Great Buddha".

Fish and rice are the most important foods in Japan. There are many fish farms inland as well as fishing at sea.

Japanese cooks make soup from shark fins.

Festivals
The Japanese people celebrate lots of festivals each year: some are specially about children. There is usually a colourful procession like this.

Shikoku

Okayama

Temple

Hiroshima

Kyūshū

Fukuoka

Kitakyushu

Nagasaki

East
China
Sea

China

China is the third biggest country in the world and nearly one quarter of all the people in the world live here. Most people live in the valleys of the big rivers and along the coast.

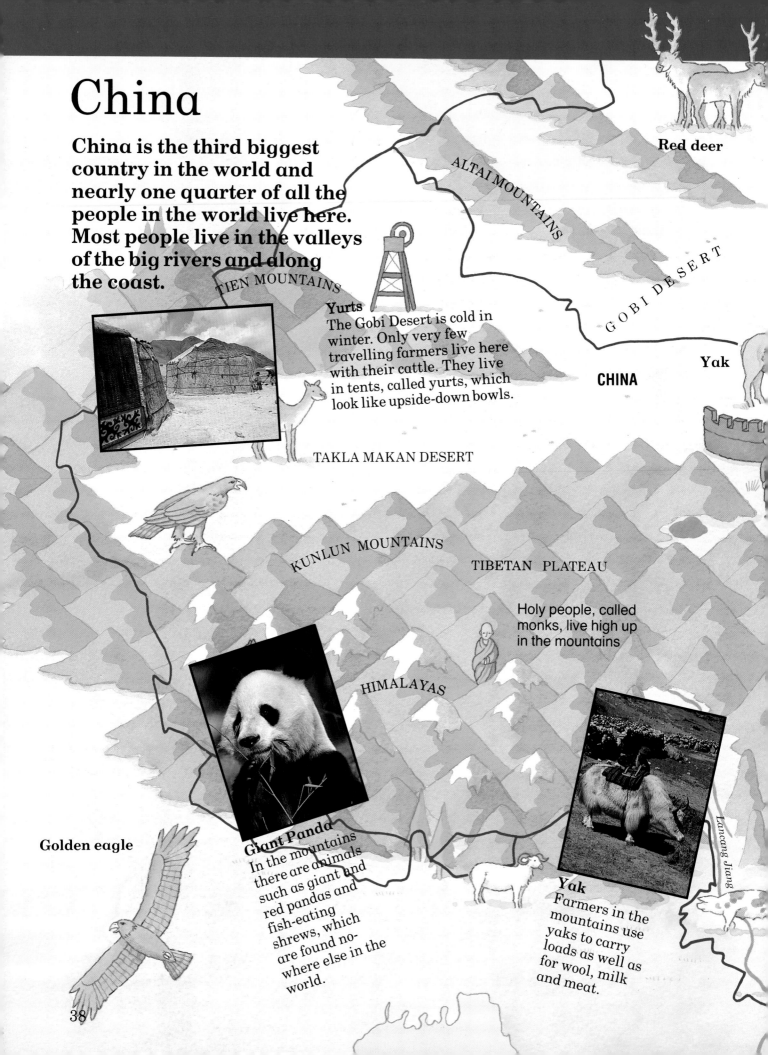

Red deer

ALTAI MOUNTAINS

GOBI DESERT

CHINA

Yak

TIEN MOUNTAINS

Yurts
The Gobi Desert is cold in winter. Only very few travelling farmers live here with their cattle. They live in tents, called yurts, which look like upside-down bowls.

TAKLA MAKAN DESERT

KUNLUN MOUNTAINS

TIBETAN PLATEAU

Holy people, called monks, live high up in the mountains

HIMALAYAS

Golden eagle

Giant Panda
In the mountains there are animals such as giant and red pandas and fish-eating shrews, which are found nowhere else in the world.

Yak
Farmers in the mountains use yaks to carry loads as well as for wool, milk and meat.

Lancang Jiang

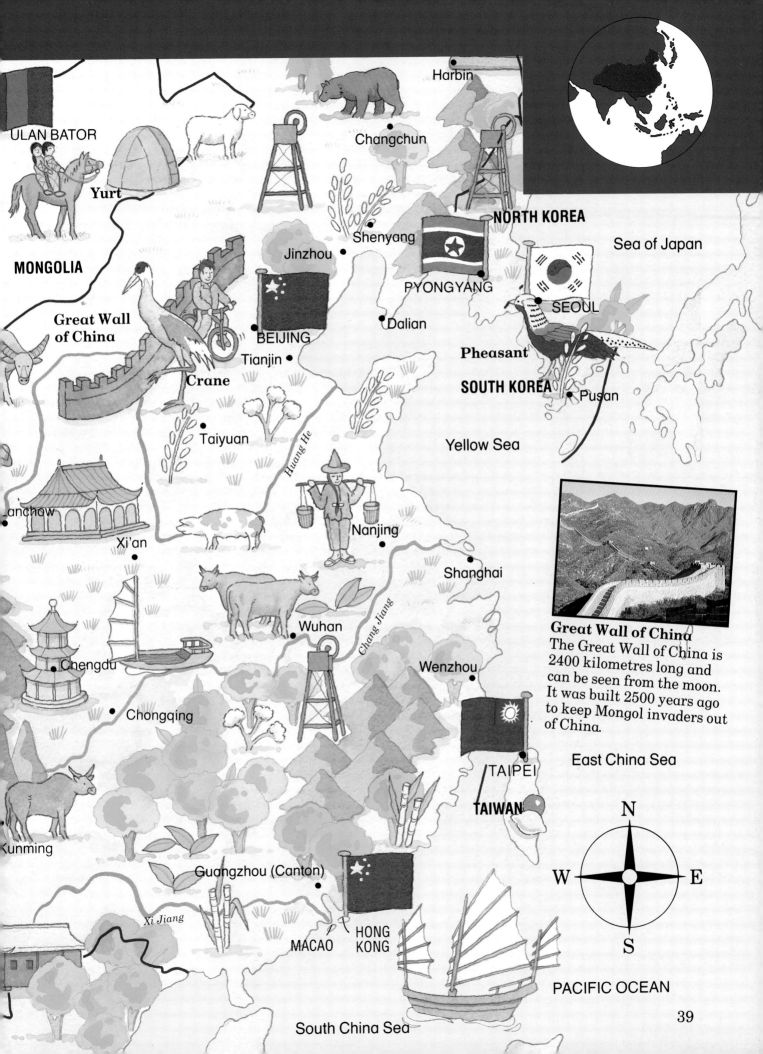

Harbin

Changchun

ULAN BATOR

Yurt

MONGOLIA

Great Wall
of China

Crane

Shenyang

Jinzhou

BEIJING

Tianjin

NORTH KOREA

Sea of Japan

PYONGYANG

Dalian

SEOUL

Pheasant

SOUTH KOREA

Pusan

Yellow Sea

Taiyuan

Huang He

Nanjing

Shanghai

anchow

Xi'an

Wuhan

Chang Jiang

Wenzhou

Chengdu

Chongqing

Great Wall of China
The Great Wall of China is
2400 kilometres long and
can be seen from the moon.
It was built 2500 years ago
to keep Mongol invaders out
of China.

East China Sea

TAIPEI

TAIWAN

Kunming

N

W   E

S

Guangzhou (Canton)

Xi Jiang

MACAO

HONG
KONG

PACIFIC OCEAN

South China Sea

39

Australia and New Zealand

Australia is the smallest continent in the world and it is completely surrounded by sea. The native people of Australia are Aborigines but 90 per cent of the population have come from Europe.

New Zealand lies to the south-east of Australia in the Pacific Ocean. It is made up of two main islands: North and South Island.

Darwin

Timor Sea

Koala

NORTHERN TERRITORY

GREAT SANDY DESERT

WESTERN AUSTRALIA

MACDONNELL RANG

Alice Springs

Ayers Rock

The Outback is the hot, dry land in the centre of Australia. Very few people live here.

GREAT VICTORIA DESERT

SOUTH AUSTRALIA

Sheep-shearing

Black swan

• Perth

NULLARBOR PLAIN

Nullarbor Plain is a huge desert plateau and is crossed by the longest stretch of straight railway in the world.

Aborigines
Aborigines paint on rocks, bark and their own bodies. Some still live by hunting animals and gathering plants.

INDIAN OCEAN

Platypus
Though a mammal, the platypus lays eggs. It lives in streams and lakes in eastern Australia.

Merino sheep
Sheep are farmed in huge farms and Australia is the greatest producer of wool in the world.

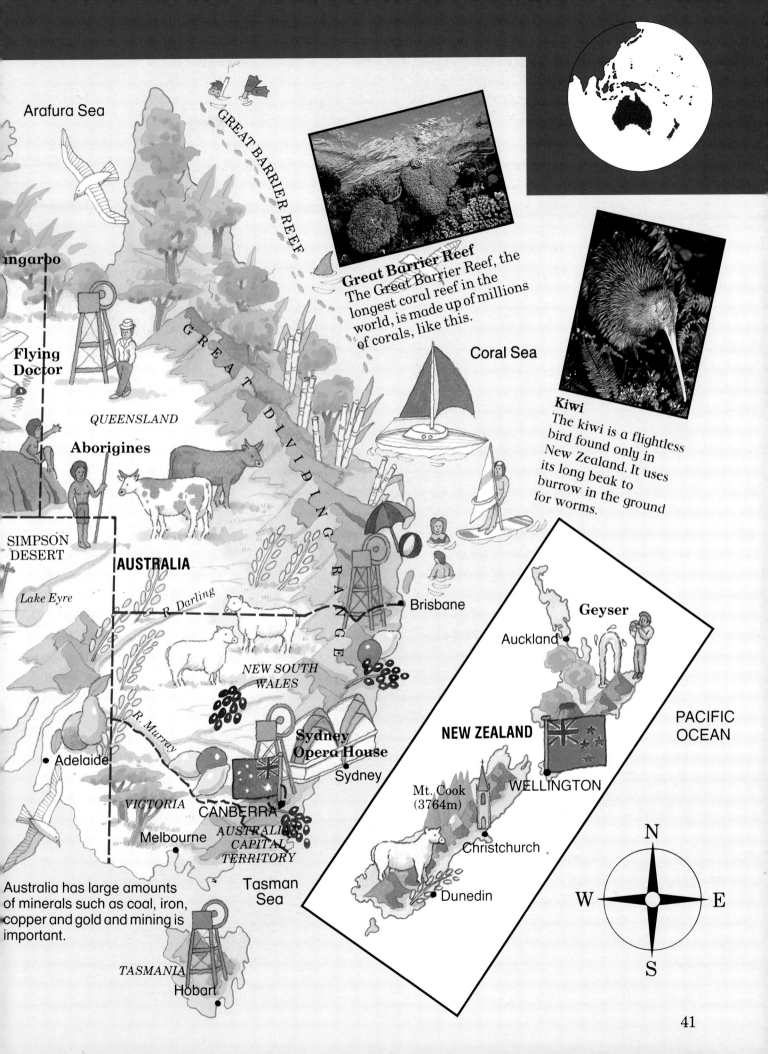

Arafura Sea

GREAT BARRIER REEF

Great Barrier Reef
The Great Barrier Reef, the longest coral reef in the world, is made up of millions of corals, like this.

Coral Sea

Kiwi
The kiwi is a flightless bird found only in New Zealand. It uses its long beak to burrow in the ground for worms.

ngarbo

Flying Doctor

QUEENSLAND

Aborigines

G R E A T   D I V I D I N G   R A N G E

SIMPSON DESERT

AUSTRALIA

Lake Eyre

R. Darling

R. Murray

Brisbane

NEW SOUTH WALES

• Adelaide

VICTORIA

Sydney Opera House

Sydney

CANBERRA

AUSTRALIAN CAPITAL TERRITORY

Melbourne

Tasman Sea

Australia has large amounts of minerals such as coal, iron, copper and gold and mining is important.

TASMANIA

Hobart

NEW ZEALAND

Geyser

Auckland •

Mt. Cook (3764m)

WELLINGTON

Christchurch

• Dunedin

PACIFIC OCEAN

N
W   E
S

41

The Arctic

The Arctic is at the very north of the world, inside an imaginary circle called the Arctic Circle. Most of the Arctic is sea, which is surrounded by the northernmost parts of Canada, Alaska, the Russian Federation, Finland, Sweden, Norway and Greenland.

Polar Bear
Polar bears live in the Arctic and hunt for seals to eat.

The correct names for Eskimos are Inuits or Yupiks depending on where they live.

Alaska (U.S.A.)

Caribou

Beaufort Sea

Reindeer

Walrus

Igloo
Many Inuits used to live in igloos, homes made out of blocks of ice. Some still do, but nowadays, most of them live in log cabins.

CANADA

Victoria I.

Narwhal

Former U.S.S.R.

ARCTIC OCEAN

NORTH POLE

ARCTIC CIRCLE

Ellesmere I.

Baffin I.

Baffin Bay

Greenland (DENMARK)

Arctic fox

Ptarmigan

Greenland sea

Barents Sea

NORWAY

SWEDEN

FINLAND

ICELAND

Greenland belongs to Denmark and is the largest island in the world.

Coal, oil and natural gas have been found under the land and sea. Pipelines take gas and oil south to warmer areas to be worked on.

Walrus
The freezing Arctic seas are the home of walruses as well as whales, seals and the narwhal.

42

The Antarctic

The Antarctic is the coldest, stormiest place in the world. It is the area around the South Pole inside the Antarctic Circle. Most of the Antarctic is a large continent, called Antarctica, which is covered by ice 2.5 kilometres thick.

ATLANTIC OCEAN

Like the North Pole, the South Pole is light all the time in summer and dark all the time in winter. It is summer in the Antarctic when it is winter in the Arctic.

Icebreaker
Icebreakers are needed to bring supplies to the scientists working in research stations.

INDIAN OCEAN

ANTARCTIC CIRCLE

Ice breaker

Seals

ANTARCTICA

Weddell Sea

RONNE ICE SHELF

ANTARCTIC PENINSULA

PACIFIC OCEAN

The first man to reach the South Pole was the Norwegian, Roald Amundsen, in 1911.

SOUTH POLE

In winter the temperature at the South Pole is −57°C and in summer it only warms up to −30°C.

ROSS ICE SHELF

Penguins

Ross Sea

Petrel

Storm petrel
Petrels nest in the cliffs around the coasts of Antarctica.

The only people living in Antarctica are scientists who work in research stations.

Penguin and chicks
There are flocks of penguins all round the Antarctic coast.

43

Pacific Islands

The Pacific Ocean covers about a third of the surface of the earth. There are thousands of islands in the Pacific which are in three main groups: Melanesia, Micronesia and Polynesia.

Pacific Ring of Fire
The Pacific Ocean is almost surrounded by volcanoes and they are often called the Pacific Ring of Fire.

Frigate bird

Wake I.

Johnston I.

Turtle

MICRONESIA

MELANESIA

Guam

PALAU

Caroline Is.

FEDERAL STATES OF MICRONESIA

MARSHALL ISLANDS

NAURU

Gilbert Is.

KIRIBATI

TUVALU

PAPUA NEW GUINEA

SOLOMON ISLANDS

FIJI

WESTERN SAMO

New Caledonia

VANUATU

TONGA

Outrigger canoe
Pacific Islanders fish in canoes and sailing boats which have logs fixed out to the side to help balance the boat in rough seas.

Kermadec Is.

AUSTRALIA

Outrigger

Coral Islands
Most of the Pacific islands are made from volcanoes and coral. The turquoise band around the edge of this island is coral.

I. = island and *Is.* = islands.

NEW ZEALAND

44

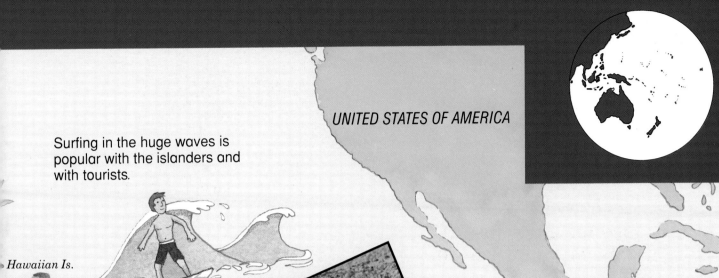

UNITED STATES OF AMERICA

CENTRAL AMERICA

SOUTH AMERICA

Surfing in the huge waves is popular with the islanders and with tourists.

Hawaiian Is.

Honolulu

Hawaii

Christmas I.

P O L Y N E S I A

Galapagos tortoise
The Galapagos Islands are the home of unique reptiles like this giant tortoise which may be up to 400 years old.

Marine iguana

EQUATOR

Line Is.

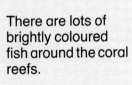

Outrigger canoe

Galapagos Is.

Samoan houses are made from the trunks of palm trees with palm leaf thatches.

Marquesas Is.

Tuamotu Is.

There are lots of brightly coloured fish around the coral reefs.

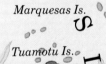

Cook Is.   *Society Is.*   *Tahiti*

Mother of pearl

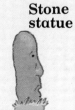

Stone statue

Stone faces
There are many giant stone statues carved out of the volcanic rock on Easter Island. No one knows who made them or what they were made for.

Pitcairn I.

Easter I.

Seal

N
W   E
S

Whale

45

Index

Names in CAPITAL LETTERS are countries

ACKNOWLEDGEMENTS

Page 12t. Barnaby's Picture Library, c. National Trust for Scotland, b. Irish Tourist Board; 13 Cadw: Welsh Historic Monuments. Crown copyright; 14 t. Bryan and Cherry Alexander Photography, c. Swedish National Tourist office; 15 t&c. Swedish National Trust Office, b. Picturepoint Ltd; 16 Picturepoint Ltd; 17 t. Bulgarian National Tourist office, b. Ardea Ltd; 18 t. Picturepoint Ltd, b. S. Bisserot/Nature Photographers Ltd; 19 J.Allan Cash Photolibrary; 20 Picturepoint Ltd; 21 t. Bryan and Cherry Alexander Photography, bl. Society for Cultural Relations with the USSR, br. Barnaby's Picture Library; 22 t. Peter Newark's Western Americana, tr. Planet Earth Pictures, b. Ardea Ltd; 23 t. Barnaby's Picture Library, b. J. Allan Cash Photolibrary; 24 t. Mexico Ministry of Tourism, bl. Oxford Scientific Films Ltd, br. Ardea Ltd; 25 t. Anne Bolt, b. Carol Lee/Black Star-Colorific; 26 Ardea Ltd; 27 tl. Picturepoint Ltd, tr. Ardea Ltd, bl. Picturepoint Ltd, br. Ardea Ltd; 28 Barnaby's Picture Library, c. Steve Pollock, bl. J. Allan Cash Photolibrary, br. Ardea Ltd; 30 J.Allan Cash Photolibrary; 31 t. Hutchison Library, b. J.Allan Cash Photolibrary; 32 Penny Tweedie/Colorific; 33 tl. Robert Harding Library, Ardea Ltd; 34 Ardea Ltd; 35 J.Allan Cash Photolibrary, cr. Ardea Ltd; 36 t. Ardea Ltd, b. Japan National Tourist Organization; 37 Japan National Tourist Organization; 38 t&br. John Cleare/Mountain Camera, bl. Ardea Ltd; 39 Heather Angel; 40 t&br. Australian Overseas Information Service, London, bl. Natural History Photographic Agency; 41 t. Ardea Ltd, tr. New Zealand High Commission, London; 42 t. Bryan and Cherry Alexander Photography, b. Oxford Scientific Films Ltd; 43 t. J.Allan Cash Photolibrary, bl. Ardea Ltd, br. Bryan and Cherry Alexander Photography; 44 t. Planet Earth Pictures, c. Picturepoint Ltd, b. Barnaby's Picture Library; 45 t. Heather Angel, b. J.Allan Cash Photolibrary.

b bottom; c centre; l left; r right; t top

Design: **Mike Pringle**
Consultant Editor: **Falcon Green**
Editorial Direction: **Tony Potter**
Art Direction: **Patrick Knowles**
Assistant Editor: **Laura Mitchell**
Picture Research: **Caroline Thompson**
Production: **Chris Atkinson**

© 1993 HarperCollins*Publishers* Ltd
First published in 1989. Updated and reprinted 1990, 1991, 1992, 1993, 1995, 1996, 1999, 2000, 2001 (twice)

ISBN 000 198363 6

Printed and Bound by Printing Express Ltd., Hong Kong.